THE PLATFORM OR THE GOLDEN APP

A Leadership Parable

Temitope Ajagbe

My Fathers House Teaching Ministries

ISBN-13: 9798300127640
ISBN-10: 1477123456

Cover design by: Art Painter
Library of Congress Control Number: 2018675309
Printed in the United States of America

CONTENTS

INTRODUCTION

Addressing the Crisis of Leadership

In today's interconnected world, where influence is wielded by churches, governments, and corporate organizations, the challenges of leadership have become more pressing than ever. Leaders face a complex web of social and ethical dilemmas, often torn between upholding their values and succumbing to the pressures of popularity, power, or profit. **"The Platform or The Golden App: A Leadership Parable"** is a story born out of this tension, offering an allegorical lens through which we can reflect on the critical state of leadership across various spheres of society.

Ethical Leadership in Churches

Churches, traditionally seen as moral compasses for communities, have not been immune to crises of leadership. Scandals involving financial mismanagement, abuse of power, and moral failings have shaken congregations' trust in their leaders. In many cases, church leaders are faced with the challenge of balancing spiritual guidance with organizational demands, navigating the line between religious conviction and public expectations.

Too often, the allure of growing congregations, mega-church fame, and societal influence diverts leaders from their core mission: serving their communities with humility and integrity.

The focus shifts from spiritual awakening to brand building, leaving behind a trail of disillusioned followers. The book's allegory resonates here, as it challenges leaders to examine the cost of compromising their principles for short-term success.

The Hillsong Church Scandal: A Crisis in Religious Leadership

In recent years, the global megachurch Hillsong faced a series of scandals involving financial mismanagement, abuse of power, and allegations of inappropriate behavior by its leadership. These revelations not only disillusioned its followers but also highlighted how the pursuit of growth and celebrity status can corrupt a church's mission.

Hillsong's leadership prioritized branding and expansion, creating a culture that often valued appearances over accountability. This mirrors the narrative in **"The Platform or The Golden App"**, where Aron Bright, the acting CEO, prioritizes the Golden App's immediate popularity at the expense of Exodus Enterprises' foundational values. The crisis underscores the need for religious leaders to reconnect with their spiritual mission and practice humility, transparency, and ethical stewardship.

Leadership Challenges in Government

Governments are perhaps the most visible stage for leadership failures. Across the globe, citizens grapple with leaders who prioritize political gain over ethical governance, perpetuate systems of inequality, and manipulate public trust to maintain power. Corruption scandals, partisan gridlock, and a lack of accountability have left many disillusioned with those elected to serve them.

The pressure to appease interest groups, secure reelection, or maintain global influence often overshadows the ethical responsibilities of governance. The result is a leadership vacuum —one where trust erodes, and society suffers. The narrative of Moses Stone and Exodus Enterprises serves as a metaphor for what happens when leaders lose sight of their purpose and the people they serve. It is a call for a new kind of leadership: one rooted in accountability, transparency, and a genuine commitment to the greater good.

The COVID-19 Pandemic and Government Leadership Failures

The global COVID-19 pandemic exposed weaknesses in government leadership across many nations. Inconsistent messaging, delayed responses, and prioritization of political gains over public health led to preventable loss of lives. For instance, the politicization of mask mandates and vaccine distribution in countries like the United States revealed a deep divide between leadership decisions and the welfare of the public.

The pandemic highlighted the dangers of leaders succumbing to external pressures, whether from political factions or public opinion, rather than acting decisively based on evidence and ethics. In **"The Platform or The Golden App"**, this dilemma is reflected in Aron's struggle to appease employees and investors during Moses' absence, leading to decisions that compromise the company's mission. The lesson is clear: ethical courage and prioritization of the greater good are essential for effective governance.

The Corporate Leadership Dilemma

In the corporate world, the pursuit of profit often takes precedence over ethical innovation and employee well-being. Companies like PharaohCorp, depicted in the book, mirror real-life monopolies that stifle competition, exploit workers, and prioritize shareholders over stakeholders. From high-profile tech giants to everyday businesses, leaders face mounting pressure to deliver short-term gains, often at the expense of long-term impact.

This environment creates a culture of compromise, where flashy products and marketing campaigns—like the Golden App in the story—overshadow the pursuit of meaningful progress. Leaders become driven by metrics and virality, losing sight of the people and values that should underpin their organizations. The book highlights the dangers of such cultural drift and the necessity for leaders to reclaim their purpose through deliberate and courageous action.

The Facebook-Cambridge Analytica Scandal: Corporate Ethics on Trial

The revelation that Facebook (now Meta) allowed Cambridge Analytica to exploit user data for political purposes was a watershed moment in corporate ethics. The scandal exposed how tech giants prioritize profit and influence over user privacy and accountability. Despite public outrage and subsequent hearings, meaningful changes to data privacy practices were slow and insufficient.

This mirrors the ethical compromises of PharaohCorp in **"The Platform or The Golden App"**, a tech monopoly that thrives on exploitation and suppressing competition. It also resonates with Aron's decision to pursue the flashy but hollow Golden App, sacrificing the company's vision of ethical innovation. The

Facebook-Cambridge Analytica crisis serves as a stark reminder of the need for corporate leaders to prioritize ethics over profit and to build trust with their stakeholders.

The Necessity for an Awakening in Leadership

Across all these domains—religious, governmental, and corporate —the underlying issue is the same: a crisis of values. Leaders are increasingly disconnected from the people they serve, and their decisions are often dictated by external pressures rather than internal conviction. What is needed is an awakening, a transformational shift in the way leadership is understood and practiced.

1. **Reconnecting with Purpose:** Leaders must re-center their decisions around the mission they set out to achieve. Whether it's spiritual guidance, public service, or ethical innovation, a clear sense of purpose is essential to navigate the complexities of leadership.

2. **Prioritizing Accountability:** Transparency and accountability are the cornerstones of trust. Leaders must create structures that hold themselves and their organizations responsible for their actions, fostering an environment of integrity.

3. **Fostering Ethical Courage:** The ability to stand firm in the face of pressure—whether from markets, voters, or societal expectations—is a hallmark of transformative leadership. Leaders must be willing to make difficult decisions that align with their values, even when it comes at a personal or organizational cost.

4. **Empowering Others:** True leadership is not about control

but empowerment. By building cultures of shared ownership and collaboration, leaders can create sustainable systems that outlast their tenure.

A Timely Parable for Leadership Today

"The Platform or The Golden App" serves as a timely reminder of these principles, presenting a story that resonates across industries and institutions. By drawing on the struggles of Exodus Enterprises, the book challenges readers to reflect on their own leadership journeys and the compromises they may have made along the way. It is a call to action for leaders everywhere to awaken to their higher purpose and to lead with integrity in an age of unprecedented challenges.

Whether you are a spiritual leader striving to inspire your congregation, a policymaker grappling with complex social issues, or an entrepreneur balancing innovation with ethics, this parable offers valuable lessons on the power of purpose-driven leadership.

THE PLATFORM OR THE GOLDEN APP: A LEADERSHIP PARABLE

◆ ◆ ◆

A parody of Exodus 32

CHAPTER 1: THE STARTUP

◆ ◆ ◆

The Rise of PharaohCorp

P haraohCorp wasn't always the juggernaut it came to be. Decades earlier, it was just another ambitious tech company, jostling for market share in a crowded industry. But while its competitors played by the rules of innovation, PharaohCorp mastered the art of domination. Its meteoric rise was fueled by a ruthless strategy: control the future by owning the tools to build it.

At the height of its power, PharaohCorp was more than a corporation; it was a force of nature. It controlled an ecosystem of patents so extensive that nearly every piece of modern technology owed a royalty to its vast intellectual property portfolio. From cloud infrastructures to cutting-edge artificial intelligence, PharaohCorp didn't just shape the technology landscape—it ruled it. Its motto, *"Where the World Builds Tomorrow,"* was both a promise and a warning.

Patents and Monopoly

The secret to PharaohCorp's dominance lay in its aggressive pursuit of patents. The company wasn't content with merely innovating; it sought to patent every conceivable idea, even those it had no immediate intention of developing. This strategy created a stranglehold on competitors, who often found themselves forced to license technology just to survive.

PharaohCorp's lawyers were as innovative as its engineers, crafting patent claims so broad they bordered on absurdity. A competitor could design a revolutionary product, only to discover that PharaohCorp owned the patent on its core algorithm, user interface, or even the method of its implementation.

The tech world grumbled about PharaohCorp's tactics, but no one dared challenge them. The company's deep pockets and legal army ensured that most lawsuits ended before they began.

The Mirage of Innovation

To the outside world, PharaohCorp marketed itself as a beacon of innovation, regularly unveiling flashy new products at glitzy tech conferences. These products were often surrounded by hype, with promises to revolutionize industries or change the way people lived and worked.

But inside the company's sprawling campuses, the reality was far grimmer. Much of PharaohCorp's workforce was relegated to maintaining and expanding its patent empire rather than working on genuinely transformative technologies. Engineers toiled on minor iterations of existing products, while the company diverted most of its resources toward stifling competition rather than fostering creativity.

PharaohCorp's true genius lay not in invention but in manipulation—of markets, laws, and perception.

The Market Forces at Play

PharaohCorp's ascent to dominance was not merely the result of its cunning strategies but the fortunate alignment of market forces that seemed tailor-made to propel it forward. In the chaotic churn of the tech industry, startups sprouted like weeds —ambitious, energetic, but fragile. No single competitor could mount a sustained challenge to PharaohCorp's towering presence. When a promising new company emerged, PharaohCorp pounced, acquiring the upstart with an offer too lucrative to refuse. Talent was absorbed, innovative ideas were shelved, and disruptive technologies that could threaten PharaohCorp's supremacy quietly disappeared into its vaults, never to see the light of day.

The company's grip extended far beyond the competition. PharaohCorp understood that the true battle was fought in the invisible backbone of the industry: the supply chain. With cold precision, it invested heavily in strategic partnerships with manufacturers and suppliers, securing exclusive contracts that locked smaller companies out. For many, scaling their operations without bending to PharaohCorp's terms became an impossibility. Suppliers, eager for the stability of PharaohCorp's vast orders, often severed ties with less profitable clients, further tightening PharaohCorp's stranglehold on the market.

Adding to its arsenal was the company's mastery of regulatory exploitation. While governments struggled to keep up with the dizzying pace of technological advancements, PharaohCorp capitalized on the gaps. Obscure legal loopholes became its playground, allowing it to expand unchallenged. Legislators, often baffled by the complexity of the tech world, lagged behind, leaving PharaohCorp free to set the rules of the game and rewrite them when necessary.

In this landscape of fragmented competitors, constrained supply chains, and absent regulation, PharaohCorp thrived—not as a beacon of innovation, but as a master of the system. It wasn't just a company; it was an empire, fortified by the very forces that should have checked its power.

An Empire Built on Exploitation

PharaohCorp's dominance wasn't built solely on innovation or strategy—it was propped up by the sweat and sacrifices of its vast workforce. To the outside world, the company glittered with the promise of progress, but inside its walls, a very different story unfolded. While shareholders basked in the glow of immense profits, employees paid the price.

Wages at PharaohCorp were just high enough to keep workers tethered. Entry-level positions came with glossy promises and competitive starting salaries, designed to lure in the brightest minds from across the industry. But once inside, employees discovered a ceiling that was nearly impossible to break through. Promotions were rare, and raises were even rarer. Ambitious workers found themselves running harder just to stay in place, their dreams of upward mobility quietly crushed under the weight of corporate policy.

The constraints didn't stop at pay. PharaohCorp's contracts were legendary for their ironclad clauses, binding employees to the company in ways that extended far beyond the office walls. Non-compete agreements ensured they couldn't leave for a competitor without risking legal action, while intellectual property clauses meant that anything they created—inside or outside of work—belonged to PharaohCorp. It wasn't just their labor the company owned; it was their ideas, their ingenuity, and, for many, their sense of self.

The culture inside PharaohCorp was as unyielding as its contracts. Relentless pressure was the norm, with workers expected to be available at all hours, answering emails and attending last-minute calls no matter the time zone. Failure to meet the company's punishing targets often led to swift and ruthless consequences.

"You're only as good as your last project," was an unspoken mantra, and those who faltered were swiftly replaced by the next eager recruit.

And yet, despite these conditions, people continued to flock to PharaohCorp. Its reputation as a titan of the tech world was irresistible, promising workers a chance to be part of something bigger than themselves. For many, it felt like the only way to participate in the tech revolution—even if it meant trading their freedom, their energy, and their autonomy for the chance to sit at PharaohCorp's gilded table.

The Illusion of Choice

PharaohCorp's greatest triumph was its ability to make its exploitation seem inevitable. "If you're not with us, you're against progress," the company's executives liked to say. For the average worker, there were few alternatives. PharaohCorp's control of the market meant that even those who left often found themselves using tools or platforms owned by the company.

Startups that tried to challenge PharaohCorp found themselves crushed under the weight of its legal and financial power. For most, the choice was simple: join PharaohCorp or get out of the game entirely.

The Exodus Begins

It was in this oppressive environment that **Moses Stone**, a former rising star at PharaohCorp, began to question the cost of success. He had witnessed firsthand how the company's practices stifled creativity and exploited workers, and he knew there had to be a better way.

Moses left PharaohCorp with a small group of disillusioned employees and a bold vision: to create an organization that prioritized purpose over profit, innovation over monopoly, and people over policies.

But leaving PharaohCorp was only the beginning. As Moses and his team embarked on their journey to build a new kind of company, they faced a daunting question: could they succeed without succumbing to the very forces they sought to escape?

The stage was set for an epic battle—not just against PharaohCorp, but against the compromises and temptations that threatened to derail their vision. This is where the story of **Exodus Enterprises** begins.

CHAPTER 2: THE RECRUITMENT AND FUNDRAISING

◆ ◆ ◆

The dawn of Exodus Enterprises was as scrappy and tumultuous as its mission was bold. Moses Stone, once a rising star at PharaohCorp, had envisioned a company that would challenge the oppressive monopoly and bring ethical innovation to the tech industry. However, translating that vision into reality proved to be a battlefield fraught with conflicts over hiring, funding, and survival in a landscape dominated by PharaohCorp's shadow.

The First Hire

Moses knew that the strength of his new venture would lie in its people. He didn't just need talent; he needed believers—people who shared his vision for a better, freer tech industry. His first recruit was **Aron Bright**, a distant cousin and a charismatic operations manager with a flair for building relationships. Aron had spent years working in PharaohCorp's sprawling bureaucracy, where his charm and eloquence often earned him praise, but he'd grown weary of the company's relentless exploitation.

"Moses, I'm in," Aron said during their first meeting in a crowded coffee shop. "But if we're going to do this, we need to build something people want to fight for. Otherwise, we'll never survive PharaohCorp's shadow."

Aron's ability to inspire and connect with people complemented Moses' strategic brilliance. Together, they began laying the groundwork for Exodus Enterprises, crafting a vision that could attract talent and investors alike.

The Battle Over Office Space

Finding a physical space to house their fledgling company became the first of many challenges. Moses was adamant about keeping the company close to Silicon Valley's talent pool but far enough away to avoid the prying eyes of PharaohCorp. They eventually settled on a modest office space in an industrial park—a far cry from PharaohCorp's opulent campuses.

But even this choice wasn't without conflict.

Aron, with his flair for diplomacy, argued that the office's location would send a message. "We need to show people we're serious," he insisted. "If we set up in a dingy industrial park, we'll look like amateurs. How are we supposed to attract top-tier talent if we're operating out of a glorified garage?"

Moses countered with pragmatism. "We don't need shiny offices," he said. "We need every dollar going into the Minimum Viable Product (MVP). If Libra isn't perfect, the rest doesn't matter."

Libra, the platform designed to rival PharaohCorp, was their flagship project. It promised to be everything PharaohCorp's systems weren't—transparent, affordable, and designed to empower users rather than exploit them. Moses' decision to prioritize the product over appearances set the tone for the company's culture: Exodus Enterprises would focus on substance over style.

Reluctantly, Aron conceded. The industrial park office became their headquarters, a scrappy symbol of their underdog mentality.

Libra: The Open-Source Hope

The development of **Libra** became the heart of the company's early efforts. The platform was envisioned as a modular software system that could integrate seamlessly with existing technologies, offering companies an alternative to PharaohCorp's proprietary systems.

Aron, who was less technically inclined than Moses, took charge of morale and recruitment, rallying a team of engineers and designers who believed in the mission. His charm and persuasive speeches inspired the small but dedicated group. "This isn't just a job," Aron said during an onboarding session. "It's a chance to make history. We're not building software; we're building freedom."

The team's belief in Libra kept them working through grueling hours and setbacks. "If we can pull this off," one engineer said during a late-night brainstorming session, "we'll prove that PharaohCorp isn't invincible."

The Lawsuit Storm

As word of Exodus Enterprises began to spread, so too did the wrath of PharaohCorp. It started with whispers of legal threats but soon escalated into a full-blown lawsuit. PharaohCorp accused Exodus Enterprises of patent infringement, claiming that Libra's core algorithms bore an uncanny resemblance to proprietary systems Moses had overseen during his time at PharaohCorp.

The accusations were baseless—Libra's architecture was entirely original—but PharaohCorp's legal team wasn't interested in winning the case outright. Their goal was clear: to bleed Exodus Enterprises dry through drawn-out litigation.

"This is PharaohCorp's playbook," Aron fumed during an emergency meeting. "They don't need to win. They just need to make it too expensive for us to fight."

The lawsuit also included a claim of **labor stealing**, alleging that Exodus Enterprises had poached key employees from PharaohCorp and encouraged them to violate their non-compete agreements. While some recruits had indeed left PharaohCorp to join Exodus, Moses had been meticulous in ensuring their contracts were legally sound.

"We'll fight this," Moses said, his voice steady despite the tension in the room. "PharaohCorp wants us to believe we're powerless. But we're not. We'll defend ourselves, and we'll win."

The Fundraising Gamble

To survive the legal onslaught and bring Libra to market, Moses turned his attention to fundraising. Aron, with his natural charisma, played a pivotal role in pitching to investors. Together, they presented Exodus Enterprises as not just a company but a movement—a rallying cry for those who believed the tech industry could be better.

"Why should we invest in a company that's about to be crushed by a giant?" one venture capitalist asked bluntly.

Aron, unflappable as ever, leaned forward with a smile. "Because giants always fall," he said. "And when PharaohCorp falls, the companies that stood against it will define the future. Do you want to be part of that future, or do you want to stay chained to the past?"

The pitch won over a handful of key investors, who provided the funding Exodus Enterprises needed to keep going. The money was used to bolster their legal defense, expand the development team, and prepare for Libra's launch.

A Tenuous Hope

By the end of their second year, Exodus Enterprises had survived its first major battles, but the war was far from over. The lawsuits continued to drain their resources, and PharaohCorp's shadow loomed large.

Yet, despite the challenges, there was a sense of momentum. The MVP for Libra was nearing completion, and the team's scrappy determination had begun to attract attention. Tech blogs and independent media outlets started to write about Exodus Enterprises, framing them as the *David* to PharaohCorp's *Goliath*.

Aron, reflecting on their journey, stood with Moses in the industrial park parking lot after a particularly long day. "We've got a long way to go," Aron said, his voice tinged with both exhaustion and hope. "But for the first time, I actually believe we can do this."

Moses smiled, his gaze fixed on the horizon. "We're not just building a company, Aron. We're building a future. And no lawsuit, no monopoly, no PharaohCorp is going to stop us."

As they walked back into the office, the fight for Exodus Enterprises' survival—and its mission—had only just begun.

CHAPTER 3: THE GREAT ABSENCE

◆ ◆ ◆

Moses' Departure

When Moses Stone announced his temporary departure to attend the Sinai Conference, there was a palpable mix of excitement and apprehension within Exodus Enterprises. The Sinai Conference was the tech industry's most prestigious stage, a place where visionaries unveiled ideas that could shape the future. Moses' mission was clear: to present their groundbreaking platform, Libra, to the world and secure the remaining funding needed to ensure its successful launch.

Accompanying him was **Joshua Rivers**, a sharp and steadfast operations lead who had become Moses' trusted confidant. Joshua's role was to provide logistical support while Moses focused on winning over investors and dazzling the conference audience.

"I'm counting on you to hold the fort," Moses told **Aron Bright** as they stood in the cramped industrial park office. "You're the acting CEO while I'm gone. Keep the team focused, and remind them why we're doing this."

Aron nodded, a mix of pride and nervousness in his expression. "I won't let you down, Moses. You can trust me."

With that, Moses and Joshua departed, leaving Aron to steer the ship during what would prove to be the company's most turbulent weeks.

The Acting CEO

At first, Aron relished the role of acting CEO. His natural charisma and eloquence made him a reassuring presence during team meetings, where he delivered motivational speeches and updates with confidence. "Moses is out there showing the world what we're capable of," he told employees. "It's our job to keep things moving forward."

Aron also embraced the symbolic aspects of leadership, hosting team lunches and brainstorming sessions to keep morale high. Employees appreciated his approachable demeanor, and for a brief moment, it seemed the company might weather Moses' absence without issue.

But Aron's strengths as a diplomat were soon tested by the weight of decision-making. With Moses gone, every operational question and strategic dilemma landed squarely on Aron's desk. It wasn't long before the cracks began to show.

The Whisper Campaign

As days turned into weeks, whispers of uncertainty began to spread. Moses' absence, which was initially expected to last two weeks, had stretched into its fourth, with only occasional updates trickling in from Joshua.

Rumors swirled among employees:

- "The runway is shorter than we thought," one developer confided to a colleague over lunch.
- "If Moses doesn't secure funding soon, we're done for," another whispered in the break room.
- "Why hasn't Aron told us anything? Does he even know what's going on?"

The whispers soon grew louder, fueled by a growing sense of anxiety. Employees began to question whether the company's ambitious vision was sustainable. Some started updating their resumes, while others grew resentful of Aron's perceived lack of transparency.

The Fear of Collapse

The tension reached a boiling point during an all-hands meeting when an engineer named **Leah** raised the question everyone had been avoiding. "Aron," she said, standing up from her chair, "can you tell us how much runway we actually have left? And what happens if Moses doesn't come back with the funding?"

Aron, caught off guard, hesitated for a moment too long. "We're in a solid position," he said finally, trying to project confidence. "Moses is working hard to secure what we need, and Libra is going to blow everyone away at the Sinai Conference."

Leah pressed further. "That's not an answer. We need transparency. We're the ones keeping this place running while he's gone, and we deserve to know what's really happening."

The room fell silent, all eyes on Aron. He shifted uncomfortably before giving a diplomatic response. "I understand your concerns, and I promise you, we're doing everything possible to ensure our success. Moses wouldn't be out there if he didn't believe in what we're building."

The answer satisfied no one, and the meeting ended on a somber note. The fear of collapse hung in the air like a storm cloud.

The Sinai Conference

Meanwhile, Moses and Joshua were navigating their own challenges at the Sinai Conference. The event was a whirlwind of networking, pitch sessions, and high-stakes presentations. Tech giants and emerging startups alike competed for the attention of investors and media, each vying to position themselves as the next big thing.

Moses' presentation of Libra was a highlight of the conference. Standing before a packed auditorium, he delivered a passionate pitch that outlined the platform's potential to disrupt PharaohCorp's stranglehold on the industry.

"Technology should serve people, not enslave them," Moses declared, his voice resonating through the room. "Libra is more than a platform—it's a promise. A promise that innovation can be ethical, accessible, and empowering."

The audience erupted in applause, and Moses left the stage to a flurry of investor interest. Yet, behind the scenes, the battle for funding was far from over. Many investors expressed skepticism about the company's ability to compete with PharaohCorp, citing its ongoing lawsuits and precarious runway as major risks.

"They love the vision, but they don't trust the numbers," Joshua summarized after one particularly grueling round of meetings. "We need more than inspiration. We need results."

The Boiling Point

Back at the office, Aron's attempts to maintain morale were failing. Employees, frustrated by the lack of updates, began to question his leadership. The once-cohesive team splintered into factions:

- **The Loyalists**, who trusted Moses and believed he would return with the funding needed to save the company.
- **The Skeptics**, who were convinced the company was on the brink of collapse and began quietly looking for other opportunities.
- **The Innovators**, who grew restless and proposed pivoting the company's focus to smaller, less ambitious projects that

could generate immediate revenue.

Caught between these competing groups, Aron found himself paralyzed. His diplomatic approach, which relied on consensus-building, proved ineffective in the face of mounting pressure.

During a private conversation with a senior developer, Aron admitted his doubts. "I'm trying to keep everyone together, but it's like holding back a flood with a handful of sandbags. If Moses doesn't come back soon, I don't know how much longer we can hold on."

CHAPTER 4: THE GOLDEN APP

◆ ◆ ◆

The weeks following Moses Stone's departure for the Sinai Conference were a pressure cooker at Exodus Enterprises. The company had been founded on a vision of ethical innovation, embodied by its flagship project, the Libra Platform, which promised to revolutionize the tech industry with transparency, accessibility, and empowerment. Yet, as uncertainty about the company's future mounted, that vision began to feel increasingly fragile.

The tension between **the idealists**, who remained loyal to Moses' vision, and **the pragmatists**, who saw immediate survival as the priority, threatened to fracture the team. At the center of this storm stood **Aron Bright**, the acting CEO, caught between competing demands from employees, investors, and market forces.

Mounting Pressure from the Market

Outside the industrial park office, the tech industry showed no mercy. **PharaohCorp**, with its seemingly endless resources, began rolling out aggressive marketing campaigns for its latest product—a sleek, proprietary platform eerily similar to the promised capabilities of Libra. Industry analysts speculated that PharaohCorp had caught wind of Exodus' plans and was moving to preemptively crush its upstart competitor.

Tech blogs began publishing skeptical takes on Exodus Enterprises. *'Is Libra Too Late to the Game?"* one headline read. Investors who had expressed cautious interest at the Sinai Conference grew colder in their responses to follow-up calls, their confidence shaken by PharaohCorp's overwhelming dominance.

Inside the company, the tension was palpable. Employees scrolled through their feeds, watching PharaohCorp's latest announcements with growing dread. "They're going to beat us to market," whispered Leah, the social media strategist, during a lunch break. "How are we supposed to compete with that?"

The Employee Divide

While market forces pressed from the outside, internal conflicts brewed within the office. Aron held weekly meetings to address concerns and maintain morale, but these sessions often devolved into heated debates.

- **The Loyalists**, including senior developer Ethan, insisted that the company stay the course with Libra. "We've come this far," Ethan argued passionately. "Abandoning Libra now would betray everything this company stands for."
- **The Pragmatists**, led by Leah, proposed pivoting to a smaller, faster project to generate immediate revenue. "If we don't show the market we can deliver something soon, there won't be a company left to build Libra," she said during one meeting.
- **The Skeptics**, like Martin in accounting, were openly critical of the lack of direction. "We're sinking money into a product that's not even finished while PharaohCorp eats our lunch," he said bluntly. "We need a new plan—or we need to fold."

Aron found himself paralyzed by the competing voices. His instinct was to listen, to mediate, to find a path forward that satisfied everyone. But as the pressure mounted, it became clear that he couldn't simply please the crowd—he needed to make a decision.

The Birth of an Idea

It was during one of these tense meetings that Leah first floated the idea of **the Golden App**. "What if we developed something small but bold?" she suggested. "Something that grabs attention and shows the market we're still here."

"What kind of app?" Aron asked, leaning forward, intrigued but wary.

"Something that reflects our values," Leah said, her voice growing more animated. "An app that's user-friendly, engaging, and symbolic of what we stand for. It doesn't have to be as ambitious as Libra—it just needs to make people take notice."

The idea sparked immediate debate. The Loyalists dismissed it as a distraction, while the Pragmatists latched onto it as a potential lifeline. Aron, ever the diplomat, promised to think it over.

Aron's Calculus

Over the next few days, Aron wrestled with the decision. Every fiber of his being told him to stay true to Moses' vision for Libra, but the mounting pressure—from employees, investors, and the market—made that path feel increasingly untenable. He began weighing the pros and cons with a ruthless practicality.

- **Pros of the Golden App**:
    - It could be developed quickly, providing a much-needed morale boost and demonstrating the team's capability.
    - It might generate enough buzz to attract investors and buy more runway for Libra.
    - It would unify the Pragmatists and Skeptics, who were growing restless.
- **Cons of the Golden App**:
    - It risked diverting resources and focus away from Libra.

o It represented a compromise that might alienate the Loyalists.

o It could tarnish the company's reputation if seen as a shallow, opportunistic move.

Aron spent long nights in his office, pacing back and forth as he debated with himself. "What would Moses do?" he muttered under his breath. But the more he thought about it, the more he realized that Moses' approach—rooted in steadfast vision—wasn't viable in the current crisis. Aron wasn't Moses. He had to find his own way forward.

The Decision to Pivot

After days of deliberation, Aron made the call. At the next all-hands meeting, he stood before the team and announced the pivot.

"We're not abandoning Libra," he began, his voice steady but firm. "But we need to adapt. The market is moving faster than we anticipated, and we can't afford to be invisible. The Golden App will be a symbol of who we are—something that gets us noticed while buying us time to perfect Libra."

The room erupted into a cacophony of responses. The Pragmatists cheered, seeing the decision as a win. The Loyalists looked visibly crestfallen, with Ethan shaking his head in disappointment. "This isn't what we signed up for," he muttered.

Aron raised a hand for silence. "I know this isn't the path we imagined," he said. "But sometimes leadership means making hard choices. This app will not define us—it will remind the world that we're here, and that our mission matters."

The Golden App Takes Shape

Development on the Golden App began immediately. Leah took the lead, rallying the design and development teams to create something bold and eye-catching. The app, designed as a gamified personal productivity tool, incorporated sleek visuals and a customizable user interface. It was polished, engaging, and, above all, marketable.

Aron became the project's biggest advocate, using his charisma to rally the team and pitch the app to potential investors. "This is just the beginning," he said during a pitch call. "The Golden App is a glimpse of what Exodus Enterprises can do—proof that we're innovators, not imitators."

The Cracks Beneath the Surface

While the app's development energized parts of the team, it deepened divisions within the company. The Loyalists grew increasingly disillusioned, feeling that Aron had compromised the company's core values. "This isn't why we left PharaohCorp," Ethan said during a private conversation with Aron. "We're supposed to be building something meaningful, not chasing trends."

Aron, feeling the weight of his decision, tried to justify the pivot. "It's a strategic move, Ethan. We need to survive to fight another day. Libra's still our goal, but we have to be realistic."

But deep down, even Aron couldn't shake the doubt gnawing at him. Had he made the right call? Or had he sacrificed the company's soul for the sake of survival?

The Launch

The Golden App launched to moderate success, garnering attention from tech blogs and a small but enthusiastic user base. Investors began returning Moses' calls, intrigued by the app's potential. For a moment, it seemed Aron's gamble had paid off.

But beneath the surface, the company remained fractured. The Golden App had bought time, but at what cost? As whispers of

Moses' impending return began to circulate, Aron couldn't help but wonder how his cousin would react to the new direction. Would Moses see the app as a necessary adaptation—or as a betrayal of everything they had built?

The answer, Aron knew, would determine not just his future, but the future of Exodus Enterprises.

Delight and Complacency

The app's success brought an intoxicating sense of delight to the team. Parties were held to celebrate milestones. The break room buzzed with laughter as employees tested new features and competed in the app's mini-games. Aron, watching from the sidelines, felt a surge of pride. For the first time since Moses' departure, the company felt united and happy.

But the unity was superficial. The excitement surrounding the app masked deeper fractures within the organization. The Cynics, who had been skeptical of the company's mission from the start, now openly mocked Moses' vision. "Who needs a ten-year plan when you've got a hit app?" Martin joked during a lunch break.

The Innovators, emboldened by the app's popularity, began to question whether the company even needed Moses at all. "Why are we waiting for him to come back with his commandments?" Leah asked. "We've already proven we can succeed on our own."

CHAPTER 5: THE PHILOSOPHER RETURNS

◆ ◆ ◆

T he buzz in the office reached a fever pitch as word spread that Moses Stone was finally returning. After weeks of absence—weeks that felt like years to the overstressed team at Exodus Enterprises—the visionary CEO was coming back from the Sinai Conference. For many, his return was a beacon of hope. For Aron Bright, it was a complex cocktail of relief, dread, and resignation.

The Golden App, the project Aron had reluctantly approved and fervently championed, had become both a lifeline and a lightning rod. It had bought the company a sliver of relevance and brought temporary morale to a divided team. But it had also become a source of contention, a wedge between the company's Loyalists and those who had begun questioning its mission. Now, with Moses stepping back into his role, Aron would have to account for his decisions.

Aron's Psychological Relief

When Moses walked through the doors of the industrial park office, Aron's initial reaction was an overwhelming sense of relief. The weight he had carried as acting CEO—the sleepless nights, the tense meetings, the constant calculations about how to keep the company afloat—lifted, if only slightly.

"Welcome back," Aron said, forcing a smile as he met Moses in the conference room. His cousin looked older, more weathered than when he had left, but his presence was magnetic as always.

Moses clasped Aron's shoulder, his piercing gaze searching his cousin's expression. "You've done well to keep things running," Moses said evenly. "I know it hasn't been easy."

Aron nodded, his throat tightening. "We've managed. But there's... a lot to catch you up on."

Moses' First Impressions

The moment Moses stepped into the open office, he felt the shift. The energy was different—less focused, more chaotic. The team was buzzing with talk of the Golden App, their excitement spilling over in casual conversations and animated planning sessions.

"Have you seen the new user reviews?" Leah said to a colleague as Moses walked by. "People love the customization features. We might even hit our next milestone faster than we thought."

Moses paused, listening, his brow furrowing slightly. **The Golden App?** It hadn't been on the roadmap when he left. He made a mental note to dig deeper, his instincts telling him that this "new milestone" was likely a detour from their mission.

The Disappointment Sets In

Later that day, Moses and Aron sat down for a private debrief. Aron laid out the timeline of events: the market pressures, the growing unrest among employees, the divide between Loyalists and Pragmatists, and the decision to pivot to the Golden App.

"It wasn't an easy call," Aron admitted, his voice defensive but tinged with vulnerability. "But we needed something. The runway was shrinking, the team was fracturing, and morale was at rock bottom. The Golden App brought people together, gave them something to believe in."

Moses listened in silence, his expression unreadable. When Aron finished, he leaned back in his chair and exhaled slowly. "Aron," he began, his tone measured but heavy, "do you know why we left PharaohCorp?"

"Of course," Aron said quickly. "Because we wanted freedom, innovation, purpose—"

"No," Moses interrupted. "We left because we refused to trade purpose for convenience. Because we believed that technology should serve humanity, not the bottom line. The Golden App? It's exactly the kind of shiny distraction PharaohCorp thrives on. You didn't just compromise the mission—you mirrored everything we set out to change."

Aron's stomach dropped. He had anticipated disappointment, but hearing it framed so starkly hit him like a punch to the gut. "I did what I thought was necessary to keep the company alive," he said, his voice barely above a whisper.

"And in doing so, you risked killing its soul," Moses replied.

The Tense All-Hands Meeting

Moses wasted no time calling an all-hands meeting. The tension in the room was palpable as employees gathered, many wondering what Moses would say about the Golden App, which had become a source of pride for some and a point of contention for others.

Moses stood at the front of the room, his presence commanding but his expression grave. Aron sat off to the side, his heart pounding as Moses began to speak.

"I want to start by thanking all of you for your hard work during my absence," Moses began. "I know these past weeks have been challenging, and I'm grateful for the dedication you've shown to this company."

There was a murmur of appreciation, but the room remained taut, waiting for what came next.

"I've heard a lot about the Golden App," Moses continued. "And I've seen the enthusiasm it has generated. But I have to ask you all: why are we here? Why did we leave PharaohCorp to build something new?"

The room fell silent. Moses scanned the faces in front of him, his gaze lingering on key figures like Ethan, Leah, and Martin.

"We left because we wanted to build something meaningful," he said, his voice steady but firm. "Something that wasn't just another flashy product chasing market trends. The Golden App may have brought temporary relief, but it's a distraction. It's not the mission we set out to achieve."

Leah, emboldened by the app's success, raised her hand. "With all due respect, Moses, the Golden App saved us. It showed the market we're still here. Isn't that worth something?"

Moses nodded, acknowledging her point. "It is. But at what cost? Tell me, Leah, how is the Golden App different from the products PharaohCorp uses to lure people in? How does it advance our mission of ethical innovation? Or is it just a glitzy band-aid over a deeper wound?"

Leah faltered, her confidence wavering. "It... it's a start," she said weakly.

"No," Moses said firmly. "It's a detour. And the longer we stay on it, the further we drift from what makes us different."

A Fractured Room

The meeting ended in uneasy silence. The Pragmatists looked deflated, their enthusiasm for the Golden App dimmed by Moses' critique. The Loyalists, led by Ethan, felt vindicated but uneasy about how to repair the damage. Aron sat quietly, his head bowed, feeling the full weight of his decisions.

Afterward, Moses pulled Aron aside. "You're not PharaohCorp, Aron," he said, his tone softer now. "You're better than that. But you have to stop thinking like them. Leadership isn't about surviving—it's about guiding, even when it's hard."

Aron nodded, tears stinging his eyes. "I wanted to protect what we built," he said. "I didn't know how else to do it."

"Now you do," Moses said. "Let's get back on track. Together."

Reclaiming the Mission

The days that followed were tense but transformative. Moses worked tirelessly to steer the company back toward its original vision, starting with a renewed focus on the **Libra Platform**. He reassured employees that their efforts on the Golden App wouldn't go to waste but would be repurposed to align with the company's mission.

Aron, humbled but determined, took an active role in rebuilding trust with the team. He led discussions about how to learn from the Golden App's successes and failures, using the experience as a rallying point for a stronger, more united Exodus Enterprises.

The scars of the Golden App lingered, but so did the lessons it had taught. As the team refocused on Libra, they carried with them a renewed understanding of their purpose—and a deeper appreciation for the delicate balance between survival and integrity. Moses' return had been a reckoning, but it also marked the beginning of a new chapter, one grounded in the values that had brought them together in the first place.

CHAPTER 6: DELEGATION GONE WRONG

◆ ◆ ◆

The fallout from the Golden App continued to cast a long shadow over Exodus Enterprises. While the project had momentarily energized the company and garnered market attention, it had also exposed deep fractures in leadership, priorities, and alignment. At the heart of this crisis stood Aron Bright, the acting CEO during Moses Stone's absence, whose decisions had both rallied and divided the company. What began as a temporary appointment had turned into a cautionary tale of misplaced trust and unchecked authority.

A Divided Board

The board of directors had grown increasingly uneasy about the company's direction. While Moses had returned to steady the ship, the board was not convinced that Aron could remain a part of the leadership team. His handling of the Golden App debacle— prioritizing short-term popularity over long-term purpose—had become a flashpoint for debate.

During a tense board meeting, the divide became clear.

"He made decisions without proper oversight," one board member said. "The Golden App was a distraction at best and a betrayal of the mission at worst."

Another, more sympathetic to Aron, countered, "But it bought us time. Without it, we might not even have a company left."

Moses, seated quietly at the head of the table, listened intently. His loyalty to Aron was clear—after all, Aron had been there from the beginning, helping to build Exodus Enterprises. But even Moses couldn't ignore the growing pressure to act.

"If we let this slide," the chairwoman of the board said firmly, "we're setting a precedent. Leadership must be accountable, no matter who they are."

Aron's Missteps

Aron, for his part, had tried to redeem himself. In the weeks following Moses' return, he threw himself into rebuilding trust with the team, spearheading morale-boosting initiatives and supporting the renewed focus on the **Libra Platform**. But the scars of his decisions during Moses' absence remained visible.

Employees whispered about his leadership during the Golden App era. "He cared more about being liked than doing what was right," one developer said in confidence. "He ignored the mission to keep people happy."

Even Aron's natural charisma, which had once rallied the team, began to feel hollow. His attempts to defend his decisions often came across as defensive rather than reflective. "I did what I thought was necessary," he said during a heated leadership meeting. "If I hadn't, we might not even be here."

But the more he tried to justify his actions, the more isolated he became. The board saw his defensive posture as a sign that he wasn't prepared to acknowledge the full weight of his mistakes.

The Board's Decision

The final decision came during a closed-door meeting. The board, after weeks of deliberation and consultation with Moses, voted to remove Aron from his leadership role. While Moses had argued for giving Aron another chance, the majority felt that his continued presence in leadership posed a risk to the company's future.

"I understand the board's perspective," Moses said quietly, addressing the group after the vote. "But I hope we can handle this with dignity. Aron has contributed to this company in ways that can't be ignored. Let's not let his mistakes overshadow everything he's done."

The board agreed, and the task of delivering the news fell to Moses.

The Firing

Moses asked Aron to meet him in the conference room late one evening, long after most employees had gone home. The room was quiet, the atmosphere heavy with unspoken words.

"Aron," Moses began, his voice steady but tinged with sadness, "we need to talk about your role here."

Aron's expression shifted—he had known this conversation was coming, but hearing it still felt like a blow. "I assume this isn't about a promotion," he said, forcing a wry smile.

Moses didn't return the humor. "The board has decided that it's time for a change in leadership," he said plainly. "They've asked for your resignation."

Aron leaned back in his chair, his face a mix of anger and resignation. "So that's it?" he said, his voice rising. "One mistake, and I'm out? After everything I've done for this company?"

"It's not just one mistake," Moses replied calmly. "It's about accountability. The Golden App, the lack of oversight, the way you handled the team—it's not about blame, Aron. It's about trust. And right now, the board believes that trust has been broken."

Aron shook his head, his frustration boiling over. "You were gone, Moses. You weren't here to see how hard it was. I did what I thought was best. And now I'm being punished for it."

Moses leaned forward, his tone softening. "I know you did what you thought was right. And I know how much you care about this company. But leadership isn't just about making decisions—it's about owning the consequences. This isn't the end for you, Aron. It's a chance to learn, to grow."

Aron said nothing for a long moment, staring at the table. Finally, he nodded, his voice barely above a whisper. "I guess I should've seen this coming."

The Aftermath

Aron's departure sent ripples through Exodus Enterprises. For some employees, it felt like justice—a necessary step to rebuild the company's integrity. For others, it was a bittersweet moment, a reminder of the thin line between success and failure in leadership.

Moses addressed the team the next day, announcing the change with his characteristic transparency. "Aron Bright has stepped down from his leadership role," he said. "While we acknowledge the challenges we've faced, we also recognize Aron's contributions to this company. His efforts have been instrumental in getting us to where we are today."

The room was silent, the weight of the announcement hanging heavy. But as the team returned to their work, a new sense of focus began to take hold. The lessons of the Golden App era had not been forgotten—they had become the foundation for a stronger, more aligned Exodus Enterprises.

For Aron, the journey wasn't over. As he packed his office, he couldn't help but reflect on what had gone wrong—and what he could have done differently. Though his time at Exodus

Enterprises had ended, the experience would shape the leader he would become. And for Moses, the decision to let Aron go was a painful reminder of the cost of leadership, a cost he was determined to bear for the sake of the company's future.

The Cost of Abdication

As Moses reviewed the fallout from the Golden App era, one theme emerged: **delegation had turned into abdication.** Aron had delegated authority without providing guidance, and in doing so, he had relinquished his responsibility as a leader.

In a candid conversation with Moses, Aron admitted his missteps. "I thought I was empowering the team," he said. "But I see now that I was just avoiding the hard decisions. I didn't want to be the bad guy."

Moses listened patiently before responding. "Empowerment is important, Aron. But it's not the same as abandonment. True delegation means setting clear expectations, providing support, and holding people accountable. You didn't delegate leadership; you abdicated it."

The Broken Feedback Loop

Another critical failure was the absence of a feedback loop. Aron had created a culture where dissenting voices were silenced or ignored. Loyalists like Ethan and Naomi, who had tried to warn Aron about the dangers of the Golden App, were brushed aside in favor of louder, more enthusiastic voices.

"Every time we tried to raise concerns, Aron would say, 'Let's not kill the momentum,'" Ethan recalled. "It felt like he was more interested in keeping everyone happy than in doing what was right."

Without honest feedback, Aron had no way of knowing when the project was veering off course. By the time the Golden App's flaws became apparent, it was too late to course-correct.

Moses' Intervention

The fallout from **Aron Bright's** dismissal reverberated through the halls of **Exodus Enterprises** like an aftershock. While the board's decision had been decisive, its emotional toll on the company—and on Moses Stone himself—was undeniable. Aron had been more than just a colleague; he was family, a partner in the vision that had birthed the company. Now, Moses was left to pick up the pieces, not just for the team but for Aron as well.

A Fractured Team

Aron's departure left a void in the leadership team that was felt almost immediately. While many employees acknowledged the necessity of the decision, others struggled with the abruptness of the change. Aron, for all his missteps, had been a charismatic figure who had built personal connections across the company.

The marketing department, which had often been Aron's closest ally, was particularly shaken. Leah, the team's strategist, expressed her concerns during a one-on-one with Moses. "Aron made mistakes," she admitted, "but he also kept us motivated when things were falling apart. Now, it feels like we're drifting."

Even the developers, who had often clashed with Aron over the Golden App, felt uneasy. "It's not about whether he deserved it," Jason, a junior developer, said quietly during a team meeting. "It's about what happens next. Who's going to step up now?"

Moses, sensing the cracks forming in the company's morale, knew he couldn't let this divide them further. Aron's firing had been necessary, but it couldn't become the narrative that defined Exodus Enterprises.

A Personal Reckoning

Late one night, as Moses sat in his office poring over notes from the day's meetings, he found himself replaying the conversation with Aron in his mind. The anger in Aron's voice, the frustration in his eyes, lingered like a ghost.

Had he done enough to prepare Aron for the pressures of leadership? Had he allowed the weight of the company's struggles to fall too heavily on his cousin's shoulders? These questions gnawed at Moses, even as he reassured himself that the decision had been the right one.

He finally reached for his phone and called Aron. The line rang for what felt like an eternity before Aron answered, his tone curt. "Moses," he said. "What do you want?"

"I want to talk," Moses replied. "Not as your boss, but as your cousin. Can we meet?"

After a pause, Aron sighed. "Fine. Tomorrow. Coffee shop on Fifth. Eight o'clock."

The Intervention

The next morning, Moses arrived early, sitting at a corner table with two steaming cups of coffee. When Aron walked in, his usual confident stride was replaced by a slower, more subdued gait. He sat down without a word, his expression guarded.

"Aron," Moses began, "I know you're angry. And you have every right to be. But I need you to understand—this wasn't about punishing you. It was about protecting the company."

Aron's jaw tightened. "Protecting the company? By throwing me under the bus? I was doing the best I could with what I had, Moses. You weren't here. You didn't see how hard it was."

"I know," Moses said softly. "And I take responsibility for that. I left you in an impossible situation, and I didn't give you the support you needed. That's on me. But Aron, leadership isn't just about doing your best—it's about owning the outcome, even when it doesn't go your way."

Aron looked away, his frustration giving way to something closer to sorrow. "I thought I was helping," he said quietly. "But all I did was make things worse."

"You didn't fail," Moses said, leaning forward. "You made decisions that you thought were right. Some of them worked, some didn't. But that doesn't define you. What defines you is what you do next."

Rebuilding Trust

Their conversation marked the beginning of a fragile but hopeful reconciliation. Moses offered Aron a chance to contribute to the company in a different capacity, not as a leader but as an advisor —someone who could provide insights without the pressures of decision-making.

"I need your perspective, Aron," Moses said. "You understand this team in ways I don't. But it has to be on different terms. No titles, no expectations—just your honest feedback."

Aron hesitated before nodding. "I'll think about it."

Back at the office, Moses addressed the leadership team. "Aron's departure was a turning point," he said. "But it's not the end of his story—or ours. We have to take the lessons we've learned and use them to move forward, stronger and more aligned than ever."

The Road Ahead

The fallout from Aron's firing didn't dissipate overnight. But

Moses' willingness to confront the emotional weight of the decision, both for Aron and the team, began to rebuild trust. By framing the event not as a failure but as a necessary course correction, he helped the company refocus on its mission.

For Aron, the road to redemption was just beginning. While he no longer held a leadership role, his contributions to Exodus Enterprises took on new meaning. And for Moses, the experience served as a stark reminder of the burden of leadership—and the resilience it required to carry both the company and its people forward.

CHAPTER 7: THE TYRANNY OF CULTURE

◆ ◆ ◆

The Golden App era at Exodus Enterprises left more than fractured teams and misaligned priorities; it fundamentally altered the company's culture. Aron Bright's leadership approach had unwittingly allowed a toxic strain of groupthink to take root—a culture where the loudest voices dictated the narrative and where fleeting trends overshadowed timeless principles. The tyranny of contemporary culture, unchecked and unmoored from the company's original mission, became one of the greatest challenges Moses Stone faced upon his return.

The Rise of Fickle Culture

During Aron's tenure as Acting CEO, the Golden App became more than just a project—it became a symbol of a new cultural ethos. Employees celebrated not just the app but what it represented: creativity without boundaries, instant gratification, and the belief that popularity equaled success.

"Aron made it fun to work here," Leah, the social media strategist, explained during a town hall. "For the first time, we felt like we could try anything without worrying about whether it was 'on brand' or 'on mission.'"

But the freedom Aron had fostered came at a cost. In the absence of clear guidelines or a unifying vision, the company's culture became a patchwork of competing values. Teams prioritized what was trendy over what was meaningful, and employees began measuring success by how much attention their work received rather than by its impact.

The Seduction of Popularity

The Golden App had left more than just a dent in **Exodus Enterprises'** vision—it had reshaped the company's perception of success in ways that threatened its core values. As excitement over the app's initial reception faded, a damaging idea took root: popularity was the ultimate metric of achievement. This mindset, subtle at first, began to permeate every level of the organization, steering it further from the mission Moses Stone had so carefully cultivated.

In **Marketing**, the shift was most apparent. Campaigns became increasingly focused on virality, with substance taking a backseat to spectacle. The unspoken mantra, "If it doesn't get clicks, it doesn't matter," drove the team to chase trends rather than craft meaningful messaging. Leah, the team's strategist, justified it as "giving the people what they want," but in truth, they were losing sight of what the company stood for.

The **Product Teams** followed suit. Features that were flashy and marketable began to take precedence over solving real problems. During one brainstorming session for an unrelated project, Jason, a junior developer, casually suggested adding gamification. "It worked for the Golden App," he argued. His colleagues nodded, more interested in replicating the app's surface-level success than addressing user needs. Practicality and purpose were sacrificed on the altar of immediate appeal.

Even **Leadership**, once the bedrock of the company's purpose-driven ethos, hesitated to challenge the new direction. Aron Bright, who had always prided himself on his ability to balance competing priorities, found himself swept up in the cultural tide. Fearful of alienating employees or dampening morale, he refrained from questioning popular ideas. His silence only reinforced the growing belief that popularity equaled progress.

Moses Stone, returning from his absence, observed this shift with growing concern. During a leadership retreat, he described it as the **"tyranny of culture."** Standing before the group, he spoke with quiet intensity. "When we let culture dictate our direction," he warned, "we lose control of our destiny. A strong culture serves the mission, not the other way around. If we allow this to continue, we won't just lose our way—we'll lose who we are."

His words landed heavily, but the damage had already been done. The Golden App's legacy wasn't just a product—it was a mindset, one that would take time and effort to undo. And as Moses looked out at his team, he knew the road to reclaiming their purpose would be long and fraught with hard decisions.

The Cost of Conformity

The tyranny of culture also bred conformity. Employees who questioned the Golden App or its impact were labeled as "out of touch" or "resistant to change." This dynamic silenced dissenting voices, creating an echo chamber where bad ideas went unchallenged.

Ethan, the senior developer, recalled how he was dismissed when he raised concerns about the app. "I pointed out that the app didn't align with our mission, and someone said, 'Not everything has to be about the mission.' That was the moment I realized how far we'd strayed."

The culture of conformity stifled innovation and critical thinking.

Teams became more concerned with fitting in than with doing what was right, and the company's reputation as a leader in ethical innovation began to erode.

Moses Confronts the Cultural Drift

Upon his return to **Exodus Enterprises**, **Moses Stone** wasted no time confronting the cultural drift that had taken hold during his absence. The fractures were evident everywhere he looked—in the team's priorities, in their conversations, and most painfully, in their collective sense of purpose. Determined to reclaim the company's identity, Moses called for an emergency leadership summit.

The conference room was silent as Moses stood before the leadership team. His presence, as commanding as ever, filled the space, but there was no trace of triumph in his expression. Instead, his eyes carried a mixture of disappointment and resolve.

"This is not who we are," he began, his voice steady and deliberate. "Exodus Enterprises was founded on the principle that we would pursue what is right, not what is easy. The Golden App may have brought us together in the short term, but it did so at the expense of our soul."

Moses continued, outlining three critical shifts the company needed to make to realign with its mission.

He paused, letting the weight of his words settle. "This is not about going back to who we were before the Golden App. It's about moving forward with clarity and conviction. We've learned hard lessons, but now it's time to act on them."

The room was quiet for a moment, the leaders absorbing the gravity of the challenge ahead. Finally, Aron spoke, his voice filled with a mix of regret and determination. "I'm with you, Moses. We all are. Let's get to work."

The summit marked a turning point for Exodus Enterprises. The path to rebuilding wasn't easy, but with Moses' guidance and a renewed sense of purpose, the team began to take the first steps

The Pushback

Not everyone welcomed Moses' critique. For many employees, the Golden App represented a period of creativity and camaraderie, and they were reluctant to let go of that feeling.

"Why does everything have to be so serious?" Leah asked during a Q&A session. "Can't we have fun and still make an impact?"

Moses acknowledged the tension. "Fun and impact are not mutually exclusive," he replied. "But fun without purpose is fleeting, and impact without integrity is hollow. We must find a balance that honors both."

Others, like Martin, the senior accountant, openly resisted the changes. "This sounds like more micromanagement," he said. "You're just taking us back to the old ways."

Moses stood firm. "The old ways brought us here," he said. "The Golden App took us away from them. It's time to return to what matters."

The Cultural Reset

Moses Stone knew that fixing the fractures in **Exodus Enterprises'** culture required more than speeches and promises. To truly rebuild, he needed to realign the company's values and behaviors, creating a foundation that could withstand future challenges. Over the next few months, he implemented a series of initiatives designed to reconnect the team with the mission that had brought them together in the first place.

Values Workshops: Reconnecting to the Mission

The first step was to bring the employees back to the heart of the company's purpose. Moses introduced **Values Workshops,** immersive sessions where team members explored the core principles of ethical innovation that had defined Exodus Enterprises from the beginning.

In one session, Moses himself shared the story of how he had left PharaohCorp to create a company that valued people over profit. "We didn't start this to play it safe," he said, his voice steady but impassioned. "We started this to change the way technology serves humanity."

The workshops included group discussions where employees could share their own experiences and perspectives. Storytelling exercises encouraged them to reflect on why they had joined Exodus Enterprises and what the mission meant to them personally. By the end of each session, the room was buzzing with a renewed sense of purpose.

"It reminded me why I came here in the first place," Leah admitted after one workshop. "It's not just about what we do—it's about why we do it."

Leadership Accountability: Setting the Example

Moses knew that culture started at the top, so he made it a priority to train the company's leaders to embody and reinforce its values. **Leadership Accountability** became a cornerstone of the cultural reset.

Managers attended intensive training sessions where they were taught to model the behaviors Exodus Enterprises wanted to see in its employees. They learned how to actively challenge cultural drift, hold themselves and their teams accountable, and foster an environment where dissent and innovation could coexist.

"Leadership isn't about being perfect," Aron told a group of new managers. "It's about being accountable. If we're not living our values, how can we expect our teams to?"

Recognition of Purposeful Work: Celebrating the Mission

To reinforce the cultural shift, Moses introduced a **Recognition of Purposeful Work** program. Employees whose work aligned closely with the company's mission were celebrated in town halls and newsletters. Teams that demonstrated meaningful impact were given a platform to share their projects with the rest of the company.

One of the first recipients of this recognition was a small team of developers who had designed a feature for the **Libra Platform** that made it more accessible for users with disabilities. During a town hall, Moses highlighted their work, calling it a perfect example of what Exodus Enterprises stood for.

"This is what it looks like to align innovation with impact," Moses said, applauding the team. "You didn't just solve a problem—you made technology more inclusive. That's the kind of work that defines us."

The recognition program quickly became a source of inspiration for employees, who began striving not just for success but for success that mattered.

The Slow Healing Process

Cultural change, Moses knew, would not happen overnight. The legacy of the Golden App lingered, and some employees continued to romanticize that era. But slowly, the tide began to turn.

Ethan and Naomi, the Loyalists, took it upon themselves to

mentor newer employees, sharing stories about the company's origins and the vision that had inspired the Exodus from PharaohCorp. Leah and other Innovators began to see the value of working within a framework that balanced creativity with purpose. Even Martin, the Cynic, begrudgingly admitted that the new direction felt "more stable."

A Warning for the Future

In a company-wide address six months after his return, Moses reflected on the lessons of the Golden App era.

"Culture is like a river," he said. "Left unchecked, it can erode the strongest foundation. But when guided, it becomes a source of power, driving us forward. Let us never again allow the tides of culture to sweep us away. Instead, let us harness them to propel us toward our purpose."

The scars of the Golden App remained, but so did the lessons it had taught. Slowly, purpose began to outweigh popularity, and the company took its first steps toward rebuilding a culture that could sustain its vision for the future.

CHAPTER 8: THE THIN LINE BETWEEN FAITH AND DOUBT

◆ ◆ ◆

T he struggle to keep Exodus Enterprises afloat had reached its most precarious point. Inside the industrial park office, the air was heavy with tension as the company faced a reality no one wanted to admit: the money was running out. Paychecks had been delayed for the first time since the company's founding, and rumors of insolvency spread like wildfire among employees.

"It's just a bump in the road," **Moses Stone** assured the leadership team during an emergency meeting. But even as he spoke, the weight of their predicament pressed against him. He knew the truth: they were on the brink.

The Whispers of Doubt

In hushed conversations over coffee and quiet exchanges in hallways, employees began voicing their doubts. The once-righteous cause of Exodus Enterprises now felt fragile, precarious. For some, it became impossible not to compare their current situation to the security they'd left behind at **PharaohCorp**.

"At least at PharaohCorp, we didn't have to worry about payroll," muttered **Leah**, the marketing strategist, during a lunch break. "We had benefits, bonuses, and steady paychecks. What do we have now? Empty promises and delayed salaries."

Others echoed the sentiment. The **Loyalists**, like senior developer **Ethan**, tried to counter the growing unrest. "PharaohCorp gave us golden handcuffs," he argued passionately. "They paid well because they owned us. Do you really want to go back to that?"

But the **Skeptics** weren't swayed. "Golden handcuffs are better than no handcuffs at all," shot back **Martin**, the senior accountant. "At least we knew we'd get paid on time."

Moses Faces the Team

The tension came to a head during an impromptu all-hands meeting, where Moses addressed the company with his characteristic blend of honesty and determination. Standing before the team, he looked around at the tired, anxious faces of people who had poured their hearts into the mission.

"I know things are hard right now," he began, his voice calm but resolute. "And I know some of you are questioning whether leaving PharaohCorp was the right choice. But let me remind you of why we're here. PharaohCorp gave you paychecks, yes—but at the cost of your freedom, your creativity, and your dignity. We left to build something better, and that dream is still alive. We're just in the middle of the struggle that comes with doing something meaningful."

Leah raised her hand, her frustration evident. "Moses, I respect what you're saying, but we have bills to pay. Passion doesn't cover rent."

"I understand," Moses replied, nodding. "And I won't ask you to sacrifice more than you're able. But I will ask you to believe that this isn't the end. It's a moment—a hard one—but a moment nonetheless. We're closer than you think to turning this around."

His words sparked a flicker of hope in some, but for others, they felt like the idealism of a man out of touch with reality. The room dispersed with a mix of determination, doubt, and quiet resignation.

The Contradictions of Nostalgia

As the whispers grew louder, the contradictions in the employees' nostalgia for PharaohCorp began to surface. For every complaint about delayed paychecks, there were lingering memories of the suffocating culture they had escaped.

"I hated how they owned every idea I came up with," said **Jason**, a junior developer, during a late-night conversation with Ethan. "But now I miss the security. What's the point of freedom if I can't pay for groceries?"

Ethan sighed. "The point is that we're building something that matters. Something that won't exploit people the way PharaohCorp did. You think they're immune to struggle? They just hide it behind their shiny campuses and billion-dollar budgets."

But not everyone was convinced. For some, the reality of an empty bank account outweighed the promise of a better future. A few employees quietly began looking for other opportunities, their belief in the mission eroded by the weight of uncertainty.

The Unexpected Lifeline

Just when the tension seemed ready to boil over, a surprise email hit Moses' inbox: a **venture capital firm** that had previously declined to invest had reconsidered. The message was brief but clear—they were prepared to inject a significant amount of funding into Exodus Enterprises. The terms weren't perfect, but they were fair, and the amount was enough to stabilize the company for the foreseeable future.

Moses called an emergency leadership meeting to share the news.

The relief in the room was palpable, with even the ever-pragmatic Martin breaking into a rare smile. Aron, sitting beside Moses, exhaled deeply. "I don't know how you keep pulling miracles out of thin air," he said, half-joking.

"It's not a miracle," Moses replied. "It's faith. And persistence. They saw what we're building here, and they believe in it. Now we just have to make sure we prove them right."

Restoring Confidence

With the funding secured, Moses immediately called an all-hands meeting to deliver the news. This time, his voice carried the weight of relief and determination.

"I told you this wasn't the end," he began, his eyes scanning the room. "And I meant it. We've secured the funding we need to keep going—not just to survive, but to thrive. But let me be clear: this isn't just about money. It's about belief. Someone out there saw the value in what we're doing, and they decided to bet on us. Now it's our turn to bet on ourselves."

The room erupted in applause, a mix of relief and renewed energy. Employees who had been on the verge of leaving began to reconsider. The Loyalists felt vindicated, while even the Skeptics acknowledged that Moses had delivered when it mattered most.

A Hard-Won Lesson

As the company moved forward, Moses reflected on the struggle. The payroll crisis had been a test—not just of the company's resilience but of its values. It revealed the tension between the need for security and the desire for freedom, the allure of stability versus the cost of meaningful work.

Standing in the now-buzzing office, Moses addressed Aron privately. "This was a wake-up call," he said. "People need to believe in more than just the mission. They need to feel secure. We can't let this happen again."

Aron nodded, his usual confidence tempered by humility. "We'll get there, Moses. We'll find the balance."

And so, Exodus Enterprises continued its journey, stronger for the struggle but keenly aware of the thin line it walked between faith and doubt. The cash infusion bought them time, but it was the lessons they learned that would define their path forward.

CHAPTER 9: THE
BREAKING POINT

◆ ◆ ◆

The complaints from employees at Exodus Enterprises had become a relentless tide, crashing against Moses Stone with unyielding force. No matter how much progress the company made, the needs seemed unending, each wave carrying fresh grievances: insufficient resources, work-life imbalance, unclear priorities. For Moses, who had dedicated himself to steering the company toward its mission, the constant chorus of dissatisfaction became an unbearable weight.

The Relentless Demands

The complaints came from every corner of the company.

- **The Developers** needed better tools and additional staff. "We're stretched too thin," said Jason, the junior developer, during a heated meeting. "How are we supposed to deliver on deadlines when we're working with outdated systems?"
- **Marketing** demanded more funding for campaigns. "If we want to compete, we need visibility," Leah argued. "And visibility costs money we don't have."
- **Operations** raised concerns about burnout. "People are hitting their breaking point," Naomi reported grimly. "If we don't address this soon, we're going to see mass

resignations."

Every complaint was valid, but together, they overwhelmed Moses. His assurances, his promises to address the issues, began to sound hollow even to himself. He tried to stretch resources further, to patch holes where he could, but it never seemed to be enough.

The Breaking Point

One particularly grueling day, Moses found himself in yet another meeting where the demands piled higher than usual. The voices of his team blurred together, their frustrations amplifying his own. The room felt stifling, and his patience, normally as steady as a rock, cracked.

"Enough!" Moses' voice cut through the air, silencing the room. The team stared at him, startled. Moses rarely lost his composure, and his outburst sent a ripple of shock through the room.

"I hear you," he continued, his tone sharp. "I hear all of you. Every single day, it's more complaints, more demands. Do you think I'm not trying? Do you think I don't know how hard this is? But I can't do everything, and I can't fix everything. So unless you have a solution instead of another problem, I suggest we all get back to work."

The room fell into an uneasy silence, and Moses left the meeting abruptly, retreating to his office. He closed the door and sat heavily in his chair, burying his face in his hands. For the first time since starting Exodus Enterprises, Moses felt as though he had reached his limit.

The Violation

Desperation drove Moses to a decision he would later regret. One of the terms set by the **board of investors** was that Exodus

Enterprises would not take on debt without approval. But as the company teetered on the brink of losing key talent and missing critical milestones, Moses saw no other choice.

He quietly negotiated a **bridge loan** with a private lender, bypassing the board's authority. The funds provided temporary relief, allowing the company to purchase new equipment for the developers, expand marketing efforts, and address some of the operational concerns.

The immediate effects were positive, but the decision weighed heavily on Moses. He knew he had crossed a line, compromising his integrity to keep the company afloat. "It was necessary," he told himself repeatedly, but the guilt lingered.

CHAPTER 10: PRECARIOUS LIFELINES

◆ ◆ ◆

Amid the chaos, what seemed like miraculous lifelines emerged, but each came with its own shadow of uncertainty and risk, threatening to pull Exodus Enterprises into deeper waters rather than toward salvation.

A Fragile Partnership

An influential yet enigmatic tech firm approached Exodus Enterprises with an offer to integrate **Libra** into their systems. On the surface, it appeared to be a lifeline—promising funding and resources to ease the crushing financial strain. But buried within the fine print were clauses that gave the partner significant control over Libra's direction. "They're practically asking to own it," Ethan muttered during a tense meeting, his voice barely concealing his frustration. The decision to accept or decline became a point of bitter contention within the leadership team, testing their unity at a time when every crack mattered.

The Strings of a Government Grant

An unexpected grant for ethical tech development seemed like a godsend. It provided just enough capital to stave off layoffs, but the conditions attached were suffocating. The grant required detailed, invasive reporting on Exodus' operations, creating endless bureaucratic hurdles. "This is PharaohCorp in disguise,"

Leah complained bitterly. "We're jumping through hoops for scraps, and it's distracting us from what really matters."

What should have been moments of relief instead became reminders of how precarious their position truly was. Each lifeline felt like a temporary patch on a sinking ship, keeping them afloat but failing to address the fundamental cracks in their foundation. Moses Stone, ever the pragmatist, recognized the danger beneath the surface. These so-called blessings weren't salvation—they were delays, moments that bought time but not solutions.

"This isn't what we're building for," Moses confided to Aron one late night, exhaustion evident in his voice. "We're scrambling to survive instead of thriving on our own terms. We're tethered to everyone else's conditions when we should be setting the course."

The tension among the leadership team grew palpable as they grappled with the moral and strategic compromises these lifelines demanded. Each new opportunity came with its own subtle chains, threatening to pull Exodus further from its mission. For Moses, the bitter irony was clear: to break free from PharaohCorp, they were entangling themselves in new forms of dependence.

As the team moved forward, the realization hung over them like a storm cloud: the lifelines weren't a blessing—they were a test. Could they navigate these compromises without losing their vision? Or would these threads of salvation ultimately bind them tighter than the chains they had left behind?

A Visit from Jethro

One evening, as Moses sat alone in the office, reviewing the mounting challenges, he heard a knock at the door. It was **Jethro Midian**, a member of the board and Aron's uncle. Jethro was known for his calm demeanor and sage advice, and his unexpected visit was both a surprise and a relief.

"Moses," Jethro said as he entered, "you look like a man carrying the weight of the world."

Moses sighed, gesturing for Jethro to sit. "That's exactly how it feels," he admitted. "Everyone needs something. Everyone expects me to fix everything. I don't know how much more I can take."

Jethro nodded thoughtfully. "Do you remember the story of my namesake, Jethro, from the Bible?"

Moses raised an eyebrow, unsure where this was going.

"When Moses led the Israelites out of Egypt," Jethro began, "he tried to do everything himself—resolve every dispute, manage every task. And do you know what his father-in-law told him? 'What you are doing is not good. You will wear yourself out.' Instead, he advised Moses to appoint leaders, people he trusted, to share the burden."

Moses leaned back in his chair, letting the words sink in. "You're saying I need to delegate more."

"I'm saying you can't do this alone," Jethro said firmly. "No one can. Assemble a leadership team. Share the load. Trust the people around you to help carry the weight."

Constituting the Leadership Team

The next day, Moses called a meeting with the senior staff and shared his plan to restructure the company's leadership. He proposed creating a **leadership team**, composed of trusted employees from each department, to help make decisions and address the company's challenges collectively.

Leah, despite her earlier frustrations, became **Head of Marketing Strategy**, while Ethan stepped into the role of **Chief Technical Officer** to oversee Libra's development. Naomi was named

Chief Operating Officer, charged with optimizing processes and preventing burnout.

"This isn't about taking power away from anyone," Moses explained. "It's about empowering all of us to do better. Together, we can rebuild not just this company, but the trust and purpose we set out to create."

The team, though cautious, embraced the change. For the first time in months, there was a sense of shared responsibility—and with it, a flicker of hope.

A New Chapter

With the leadership team in place, the burdens that had nearly broken Moses began to lighten. Decisions were made collaboratively, and employees felt more connected to the company's direction. The financial struggles remained, but the company was no longer teetering on the brink.

Moses, reflecting on Jethro's counsel, realized that leadership wasn't about bearing the weight alone—it was about building a foundation strong enough to carry the load together. Exodus Enterprises wasn't just surviving; it was beginning to heal.

CHAPTER 11: THE GREAT RESET

◆ ◆ ◆

T he turmoil of the past months—the tension over the Golden App, the financial struggles, the unending complaints, and the breaking point that had forced Moses Stone to rethink his leadership—was not wasted. It had forged something stronger: clarity. Through the fires of conflict and doubt, Exodus Enterprises found its way back to the original vision, a vision centered around the Libra Platform and an audacious idea that embodied everything they stood for: the Canaan Stock Option.

This plan, long hinted at in Moses' earliest talks with employees, promised that every person who helped build the company would own a piece of it. It was a deliberate contrast to the suffocating culture of **PharaohCorp**, where workers were nothing more than cogs in the machine, their contributions swallowed up by the corporation's insatiable appetite for profit. With Libra, Moses aimed to create not just a platform, but a movement—and the Canaan Stock Option became its rallying cry.

A Vision Reclaimed

The decision to focus entirely on the **Libra Platform** crystallized during a leadership meeting in the small, unassuming conference room that had seen countless debates and compromises. This time, however, there was no ambiguity.

Moses stood at the head of the table, his voice steady and resolute. "We've learned from every misstep, every conflict, every struggle," he began. "And what we've learned is this: we lost our way because we tried to fight PharaohCorp on their terms. But we were never meant to be them. Libra isn't just a platform—it's a promise. A promise to build something better, not just for our users, but for ourselves."

The room was silent as the weight of his words sank in. Even the skeptics, those who had questioned the company's survival, found themselves nodding. The vision was clear now, sharper than it had ever been: Libra would be an open, ethical alternative to PharaohCorp's proprietary platforms, a tool that empowered rather than enslaved.

The Canaan Stock Option

At the heart of this renewed vision was the **Canaan Stock Option**, a bold initiative that would give every employee a stake in the company. It was Moses' way of ensuring that Exodus Enterprises didn't just preach empowerment—it practiced it.

During a company-wide meeting, Moses unveiled the plan. "When we started this journey, we called it 'Exodus' for a reason," he said, standing before the assembled team. "We didn't just leave PharaohCorp to escape their control. We left to create something entirely new. The Canaan Stock Option is our way of breaking free —not just from PharaohCorp, but from the very idea that workers are commodities. Here, you don't just work for Exodus—you *own* it."

The announcement was met with a mix of emotions. For some, like **Ethan**, the senior developer who had always championed the mission, it was a dream realized. "This is what we've been working toward," he said later. "A company where everyone has a stake in its success."

For others, like **Leah**, the marketing strategist who had grown weary of Moses' idealism during the Golden App era, it was a moment of cautious optimism. "I've doubted a lot along the way," she admitted. "But this... this feels real."

Juxtaposing PharaohCorp

The stark contrast between Exodus Enterprises and PharaohCorp became a central theme as the company leaned into its renewed vision. At PharaohCorp, employees were paid handsomely but owned nothing of what they built. Ideas, innovations, and even personal time were swallowed up by the corporation, leaving workers with golden handcuffs but no sense of ownership or freedom.

Exodus Enterprises, in embracing the Canaan Stock Option, flipped this model on its head. The stocks weren't just a financial incentive—they were a statement. Every feature coded, every campaign launched, every late-night brainstorming session contributed to something the employees themselves owned. It was a direct rejection of PharaohCorp's philosophy and a bold declaration of independence.

Jason, the junior developer, captured the sentiment during a casual conversation in the office. "At PharaohCorp, I felt like a number. Here, I feel like a partner. It's not always easy, but it's worth it."

The Complexities of Freedom

But with freedom came complexity. The implementation of the Canaan Stock Option wasn't without its challenges. Some employees worried about the financial implications, while others questioned whether it would truly level the playing field. **Martin**, the accountant who had often voiced skepticism, raised concerns during a leadership meeting.

"What happens if someone leaves?" Martin asked. "Do they keep their shares? And what about those of us who've been here since the beginning? Do we get more than the newcomers?"

Moses listened carefully, nodding. "These are valid concerns," he said. "And we'll address them. But let's not lose sight of the bigger picture. This isn't just about the numbers—it's about creating a culture of shared ownership and shared responsibility. If we get this right, it will redefine what it means to work for a company."

The team spent weeks hammering out the details, ensuring the plan was both equitable and sustainable. By the time it was finalized, the Canaan Stock Option wasn't just a policy—it was a testament to the company's values.

Delight in Breaking Free

As the first stocks were issued, the mood in the office shifted. Employees who had been disillusioned by the struggles of the past months found new energy in the idea that they weren't just workers—they were owners. The symbolic act of receiving their stock certificates became a moment of celebration, a tangible reminder of how far they had come.

Leah, holding her certificate, turned to Ethan with a grin. "You were right," she said. "This is what it's all about."

Even **Aron Bright**, who had struggled with his leadership during Moses' absence, found renewed purpose. In his role as Chief Engagement Officer, he spearheaded initiatives to help employees understand the value of their ownership and how it tied to the company's mission.

"This is bigger than any one of us," Aron said during a town hall. "We've built something that can't be taken away—not by PharaohCorp, not by anyone."

The Path Forward

With the Libra Platform nearing completion and the Canaan Stock Option uniting the team, Exodus Enterprises entered a new phase. The struggles of the past weren't forgotten—they became the foundation on which the company built its future.

During a quiet moment in the office, Moses reflected on the journey. The scars of PharaohCorp still lingered, but they were now reminders of what Exodus Enterprises was fighting for. Standing in the bustling office, surrounded by a team that was finally aligned and energized, he allowed himself a small smile.

"We're not just building a platform," he thought. "We're building a legacy."

CHAPTER 12: THE UNRAVELING

◆ ◆ ◆

T he dawn of what should have been a triumphant chapter for Exodus Enterprises was overshadowed by an unsettling revelation. The company had finally stabilized, with the Libra Platform nearing its much-anticipated launch, and employees had begun to believe in the dream again. But just as the team was starting to see the light, a storm loomed on the horizon —one that threatened to unravel everything they had built.

The Warning

It began with a cryptic email addressed to Moses Stone. The sender was anonymous, but the message was chillingly clear: **"You're not as free from PharaohCorp as you think."** Attached to the email were documents—internal memos, confidential contracts, and a disturbing clause buried deep within PharaohCorp's labyrinthine legal agreements.

The clause suggested that **PharaohCorp retained partial ownership of intellectual property created by any former employees who had signed certain contracts.** It was an obscure provision, likely overlooked by Exodus' legal team during its frantic early days. But if it was enforceable, it could mean one thing: **PharaohCorp had a claim to the Libra Platform.**

Moses felt his stomach drop as he read the fine print. The very platform that symbolized their freedom might still be tied to the oppressor they had fought so hard to escape.

The Board's Ultimatum

Word of the potential legal entanglement spread quickly among the leadership team and, inevitably, to the board of investors. A heated emergency meeting ensued.

"This could destroy us," said **Martin**, the senior accountant, his voice taut with anxiety. "If PharaohCorp takes us to court, we won't survive. They'll drain us dry before we even get to launch."

"We don't know if they'll act on it," Ethan countered. "This clause could be unenforceable. We need to focus on getting Libra out the door. If we back down now, they've already won."

The board, however, was less optimistic. "This isn't a gamble we can afford," one investor warned. "You need to delay the launch until we've resolved this. If PharaohCorp files an injunction, we're finished."

For Moses, the choice was agonizing. Delaying the launch could shatter the team's morale and risk losing their hard-earned momentum. But forging ahead risked the wrath of PharaohCorp— a battle they weren't equipped to fight.

The Spy Among Them

As tensions mounted, another complication emerged. An anonymous tip reached Aron Bright, suggesting that a current employee might be feeding information back to PharaohCorp. The idea of a mole within their ranks sent shockwaves through the already fragile organization.

"It's paranoia," Leah said dismissively during a private meeting with Aron and Moses. "PharaohCorp doesn't need a spy—they already have the resources to undermine us from the outside."

"Maybe," Aron replied, his tone measured. "But what if it's true? What if someone here is sabotaging us from within? We can't afford to ignore this."

The question of trust, already strained, became a fissure that threatened to tear the team apart. Subtle glances and whispered conversations created an air of suspicion that seeped into every corner of the office. Moses knew he couldn't let this divide the company, but he also couldn't shake the possibility that their enemy wasn't just external.

The Dilemma

As the launch date approached, Moses found himself at a crossroads. Three paths lay before him, each fraught with peril:

1. **Delay the Launch:** Satisfy the board by halting the rollout of Libra, giving the team time to address the legal threat. But doing so could drain morale and resources, jeopardizing their ability to recover.
2. **Push Forward:** Launch Libra as planned and risk immediate legal action from PharaohCorp. A bold move that could either solidify their independence or spell their doom.
3. **Cut a Deal:** Quietly approach PharaohCorp to negotiate a settlement. While this could neutralize the threat, it would mean compromising the very freedom Exodus Enterprises stood for—and Moses wasn't sure he could stomach that.

Each option carried its own risks, and no choice seemed free from betrayal—of the team, of the mission, or of himself.

The Counsel

Late one night, as Moses wrestled with the decision, he found himself at the office rooftop, staring out at the city lights. Aron joined him, holding two steaming cups of coffee.

"You're not going to figure this out alone," Aron said, handing Moses a cup.

"I don't see a way forward," Moses admitted. "Every choice feels like failure. If we delay, we lose momentum. If we launch, we risk everything. And cutting a deal with PharaohCorp? That's not why we left."

Aron nodded thoughtfully. "You're right—it's not. But we didn't leave just for the sake of leaving. We left to build something better. Maybe the question isn't which path is safest. Maybe it's which path lets us hold onto who we are."

The Unpredictable Twist

Just as Moses felt the weight of the decision settle on his shoulders, a startling development unfolded. A whistleblower from **PharaohCorp**—a disillusioned executive—reached out to Exodus Enterprises, offering damning evidence of unethical practices and corporate espionage within the tech giant. The information could give Exodus the leverage it needed to counter any legal threats and expose PharaohCorp's stranglehold on the industry.

But there was a catch: the whistleblower demanded full anonymity and a substantial financial reward, draining resources Exodus could hardly spare.

"It's a double-edged sword," Naomi warned during a late-night leadership meeting. "If we use this, we risk escalating the fight with PharaohCorp to a level we're not prepared for."

"Or," Ethan countered, "we show the world what PharaohCorp really is. We finally turn the tide."

The new development introduced yet another layer of complexity to Moses' already impossible decision. The clock was ticking, and the fate of Exodus Enterprises—and the very ideals it stood for—hung in the balance.

A Storm on the Horizon

As dawn broke over the industrial park, Moses stood at his desk, staring at the whistleblower's files and the latest draft of the Libra launch plan. The air was thick with tension, the weight of the decision pressing down on him like never before.

Three paths, infinite consequences.

And for the first time, Moses wasn't sure which direction to take.

ABOUT THE AUTHOR

Temitope Ajagbe

Temitope Ajagbe was born into a Christian family in Nigeria but discovered the gospel's transformative power in high school when he fully embraced the plan of salvation through Jesus Christ. Now living in the United States, Temitope is happily married to his loving wife, with whom he shares the joy of raising their three wonderful children.

With over 20 years of experience teaching Sunday school, Temitope is passionate about guiding others in their spiritual journey. He finds deep fulfillment in the critical and systematic study of the Bible, uncovering timeless principles for living a life of faith and purpose. His love for scripture and teaching shines through in his writing, inspiring readers to explore their relationship with God.